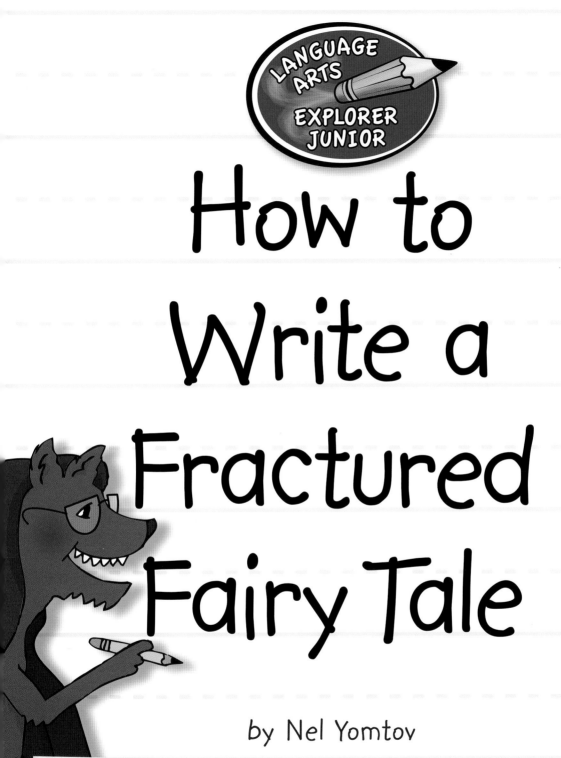

How to Write a Fractured Fairy Tale

by Nel Yomtov

CHERRY LAKE PUBLISHING · ANN ARBOR, MICHIGAN

Published in the United States of America by Cherry Lake Publishing
Ann Arbor, Michigan
www.cherrylakepublishing.com

Content Adviser: Gail Dickinson, PhD, Associate Professor, Old Dominion
University, Norfolk, Virginia

Photo Credits: Pages 10 and 19, ©Digital Media Pro/Shutterstock,
Inc.; page 15, ©Naypong/Shutterstock, Inc.; page 21, ©Andresr/
Shutterstock, Inc.

Library of Congress Cataloging-in-Publication Data
Yomtov, Nelson.
  How to write a fractured fairy tale / by Nel Yomtov.
     pages cm. — (Language Arts Explorer Junior)
  Includes bibliographical references and index.
  ISBN 978-1-62431-186-4 (lib. bdg.) —
ISBN 978-1-62431-252-6 (e-book) — ISBN 978-1-62431-318-9 (pbk.)
  1. Fairy tales—Authorship—Juvenile literature. 2. Fairy tales—Parodies,
imitations, etc. 3. Creative writing—Authorship—Juvenile literature. I. Title.

  PN171.F35Y66 2013
  808.06'63982—dc23   2013008494

Cherry Lake Publishing would like to acknowledge the work of the
Partnership for 21st Century Skills. Please visit www.p21.org for more
information.

Printed in the United States of America
Corporate Graphics, Inc.
July 2013
CLFA13

Table of Contents

CHAPTER ONE

What Is a Fractured Fairy Tale?

Do you have a favorite fairy tale? These stories usually happen "once upon a time." They have thrilled people for hundreds of years. Fairy tales always feature good characters and evil characters. In "Snow White," the dwarfs are good characters. The queen is a bad character. Many fairy tales include magical characters or items. Some of the most popular fairy tales feature kings and queens. Many have giants and monsters.

A **fractured** fairy tale is a fairy tale that has been rewritten. It alters the story of the original fairy tale to create a new one. It has slightly different

characters and locations. Fractured fairy tales
are usually meant to be funny. Anyone who's
read a fairy tale can write a fractured fairy tale.
So put on your thinking cap. Sharpen your
pencil. We're going to fracture a fairy tale!

A fractured fairy tale
fills familiar stories
with funny changes.

CHAPTER TWO

Getting Started

There are many ways to fracture a fairy tale. Think of your favorite fairy tale. How could you change it? Here are a few suggestions:

- Change the characters in the story. Snow White is normally a beautiful girl. You could make her a pig. The seven dwarfs could be mice!

- Change the setting. The setting is the location and time of your story. "Beauty and the Beast" could take place in your hometown!

- Change the **plot** or the story. Perhaps Cinderella goes to a baseball game instead of the prince's ball!

- Tell the story from a different character's point of view. Tell "Hansel and Gretel" from the witch's point of view. She can tell the reader how unhappy she was that the children were eating her gingerbread house!

- Change the **conflict** of the story. This is the main problem that drives the story along. Little Red Riding Hood's problem was that the Big Bad Wolf found her. Change the story so she is found by aliens and taken to Mars!
- Change the ending of the story. Maybe the good characters don't live "happily ever after" in your version. "Jack and the Beanstalk" could end with Jack failing to escape from the giant!

What if Jack never escapes from the giant?

ACTIVITY

Make a Chart

Do you have a favorite fairy tale? Now is the time to find one! Read a few fairy tales at your library or online. Choose the one that you like best. Then look at the chart on page 9. It shows one way to organize the parts of a fairy tale.

HERE'S WHAT YOU'LL NEED:
- The fairy tale
- Notebook paper
- Ruler
- Pencil

INSTRUCTIONS:
1. Use a ruler to help you draw six boxes.
2. Label the boxes the same way they are labeled on page 9.
3. Fill in the boxes using the information from your favorite fairy tale.
4. Make a different chart for each fairy tale you plan to fracture.

To get a copy of this activity, visit www.cherrylakepublishing.com/activities.

Sample Fairy Tale Organizer

Name: Adam Ross **Date:** March 2, 2014

NAME OF FAIRY TALE: Goldilocks and the Three Bears

CHARACTERS:	PLOT:
• Goldilocks • Papa Bear • Mama Bear • Baby Bear	Goldilocks goes for walk in the forest and comes upon a house. No one is home. Goldilocks goes inside. She tastes three bowls of porridge and sits in three different chairs. She goes upstairs for a nap and sleeps in all three beds. The bears find that someone has been in their house once they get home. They are angry. They go upstairs to look around. Goldilocks wakes up and sees the bears.
SETTINGS: • Forest • Bears' house	PROBLEM (CONFLICT): Goldilocks's problem is that she is hungry and tired. The bears' problem is that someone has entered their house, eaten their food, and slept in their beds.

CONCLUSION: Upon seeing the bears, Goldilocks jumps up out of Baby Bear's bed and runs out of the house. She never returns to the home of the three bears.

CHAPTER THREE

Mix and Match

Think hard about how you want to fracture your fairy tale.

It is almost time to fracture your fairy tale. But there's something else you might want to think about first. You can also fracture a fairy tale by mixing different stories together. You can mix and match characters and settings from different fairy tales. This will create something totally new!

You might replace the seven dwarfs in "Snow White" with the three little pigs! You could also swap settings. "The Little Mermaid" takes place in an underwater kingdom. What if you changed it to take place in the magical land of *The Wizard of Oz*. There's no limit to what you can do!

Imagine if the Tin Man climbed Jack's beanstalk!

Mix and Match

Here's a fun activity that will help you combine different fairy tales into your own fractured fairy tale!

HERE'S WHAT YOU'LL NEED:
- The fairy tales
- Notebook paper
- Ruler
- Pencil

INSTRUCTIONS:
1. Use a ruler to help you make two columns.
2. Label each column in the chart to match page 13.
3. Fill in both columns with elements from fairy tales that you know.
4. Draw a line connecting a few things from Column A to a few things in Column B. See the sample on page 13. This will give you some idea for things to combine in your fractured fairy tale.

Sample Mix and Match Fractured Fairy Tale

Name: Adam Ross

Date: March 2, 2014

COLUMN A	COLUMN B
• Rumpelstiltskin character	• The Italian village in "Pinocchio"
• Gingerbread house from "Hansel and Gretel"	• The factory in *Charlie and the Chocolate Factory*
• Cinderella's slipper	• The plot of "The Three Little Pigs"
• The Land of Oz	• Rapunzel character
• The plot of "The Boy Who Cried Wolf"	• The shepherd boy from "The Boy Who Cried Wolf"

CHAPTER FOUR

Get Ready to Write

Now it's time to get your ideas down on paper. First, you should make a long list of all the things you might want to change from the original fairy tale. For example, if you want to fracture "Cinderella," you might make the following changes:

1. Cinderella is normally beautiful. Her stepsisters are normally ugly. Make it so Cinderella is ugly. Make her stepsisters beautiful.
2. Cinderella is normally forced to do chores she doesn't like. Make it so she likes to clean and cook.
3. Cinderella normally wants to go to the prince's ball. Make her uninterested in the ball.
4. The prince is normally a great dancer. Make it so he cannot dance well.

5. Cinderella and the prince usually get married at the end. Try making it so they don't!

Did you decide to mix and match from different fairy tales? Make a long list of all the parts you want to switch around. You can mix things from as many different stories as you want. Review your list. Then decide which changes you want to include.

Make a list of all your ideas.

To get a copy of this activity, visit www.cherrylakepublishing.com/activities.

ACTIVITY

Organize Your Thoughts

You have a lot of ideas for your fractured fairy tale. This activity will help you organize them before you start writing.

HERE'S WHAT YOU'LL NEED:
- Your final ideas
- Notebook paper
- Ruler
- Pencil

INSTRUCTIONS:
1. Use a ruler to help you draw six boxes.
2. Write down the name of your fractured fairy tale. Include the name of the fairy tale you are changing.
3. Label the boxes to match page 17.
4. Fill in the boxes with the things you want to change in the original fairy tale.

NAME OF FRACTURED FAIRY TALE:
Goldilocks and the Creatures from Space

NAME OF ORIGINAL FAIRY TALE: Goldilocks and the Three Bears

CHARACTER CHANGES:	PLOT:
• Goldilocks is not a little girl. She is a professional wrestler. • Instead of bears, she meets a group of aliens from outer space.	Goldilocks goes out jogging in a park. As she turns a sharp corner, she suddenly spots a spaceship from outer space in a small clearing. She bravely enters the ship. No one seems to be inside. Goldilocks begins to work some of the controls on the ship. Suddenly, several aliens appear behind her. They are angry she has found them. Goldilocks and the aliens start to wrestle. She bumps into a control, and the ship begins to lift off!
SETTINGS: • A park in New York City • The aliens' spaceship	PROBLEM (CONFLICT): Goldilocks is in a tough spot. How will she escape the ship that is about to lift off?

CONCLUSION: Goldilocks makes a mad dash to the door of the craft just as it closes. She barely escapes and lands on the soft grass below. She promises never to go to that park again!

CHAPTER FIVE

Putting It Together

Now it's time to start writing your fractured fairy tale. Take a look at this sample. Read some of the tips on the next page before you begin.

Sample Fractured Fairy Tale

Name: Adam Ross **Date:** March 2, 2014

Goldilocks and the Creatures from Space

Once upon a time, there was a strong young girl named Goldilocks. Goldilocks enjoyed playing many different sports. But she liked to wrestle most of all. She was the top wrestler in New York City.

Goldilocks trained hard to be the best wrestler she could. She decided to go running in Central Park one sunny afternoon. The park was her favorite place to jog.

Goldilocks ran up and down many running trails. She soon found herself in a strange part of the park. She had never been there. Goldilocks soon came around a sharp turn. She saw something she couldn't believe.

It was a huge silver object. It was making a strange humming sound. A high-pitched sound squealed from beneath it. It was a giant spaceship!

"Oh my gosh!" thought Goldilocks." Where did that come from?"

Goldilocks had a brave heart and she loved adventure. She boldly began walking toward the strange craft.

You could use a computer to type your final story.

Describe your characters and settings with as much detail as you can. This makes the story more interesting. It helps create a mood for your readers. This will let them enjoy reading your fractured fairy tale as much as you've enjoyed writing it. Remember to follow the general story of the original fairy tale. Then the reader will know which fairy tale was fractured.

Finishing Your Fractured Fairy Tale

Now it is time to write out the final version of your fractured fairy tale.

HERE'S WHAT YOU'LL NEED:
- Your organization chart
- Notebook paper
- Pen
- Computer (if you want to type your fairy tale)

INSTRUCTIONS:
1. Write your name and the date in the upper right corner.
2. Write the title of your story above the first **paragraph** of your fractured fairy tale.
3. Use your organization chart to remind you what you want to include in your story.
4. Be sure to **indent** each new paragraph.

To get a copy of this activity, visit www.cherrylakepublishing.com/activities.

Share your story with your friends and family!

Great job! You've written your own fractured fairy tale. Be sure to check your work. Read it aloud. Do any sentences sound too long and wordy? Did you spell all the words correctly? Can you think of ways to improve your story?

Now you know how to write a fractured fairy tale. Which fairy tale will you fracture next?

Glossary

conflict (KAHN-flikt) a struggle or disagreement

fractured (FRAK-churd) something cracked or broken

indent (in-DENT) to start a line of writing farther from the edge of the paper

paragraph (PARE-uh-graf) a section in a piece of writing that is about a single subject, begins on a new line, and is often indented

plot (PLAHT) the main story of a fairy tale or any other work of fiction

For More Information

BOOKS

Shaskan, Trisha Speed. *Seriously, Cinderella Is SO Annoying!: The Story of Cinderella as Told by the Wicked Stepmother*. Mankato, MN: Picture Window Books, 2012.

Valentino, Jim, and Kristen K. Simon (eds.) *Fractured Fables*. Berkeley, CA: Image Comics, 2010.

Willems, Mo. *Goldilocks and the Three Dinosaurs*. New York: Balzer & Bray, 2012.

WEB SITES

Read, Write, Think—Fractured Fairy Tales
www.readwritethink.org/files/resources/interactives/fairytales
Read three fractured fairy tales, and learn how to write your own.

SlideShare—Fractured Fairy Tales
www.slideshare.net/USAteacher/fractured-fairytale
This brief slideshow explains how to write a fractured fairy tale.

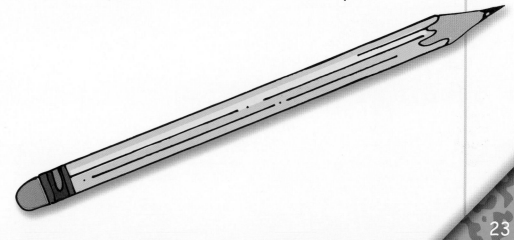

Index

About the Author

Nel Yomtov is an award-winning author of nonfiction books and graphic novels for young readers. He lives in the New York City area.